Contents

Written by
Alison Hawes
Illustrated by
Ollie Cuthbertson

Series editor **Dee Reid**

Heinemann

Part of Pearson

Characters

Salan

The King

The Lion of Jedda

Tricky words

- human
- sword
- roar
- swipes
- sling
- cloak

Read these words to the student. Help them with these words when they appear in the text.

Introduction

Salan is a slave. He wants to be free. But the evil King will only grant Salan his freedom if he can do four difficult and dangerous tasks.

One of Salan's tasks is to kill the Lion of Jedda and take the lion's skin back to the King.

THE LION'S SKIN

Salan wants to be free.
But first he has to kill the Lion of Jedda and
take the lion's skin to the King.

Salan comes to Jedda.
He sees a cave.
Outside the cave are lots of human bones.
The lion's in that cave, thinks Salan.

Salan thinks how he will kill the lion.
He gets his sword out of his bag.

Then Salan hears a roar.
The lion jumps out at him.

Salan swipes at the lion with his sword.
But it is no good.
The sword does not kill the lion.

Salan gets his sling out of his bag.
He tries to kill the lion with his sling.
But it is no good.
The sling does not kill the lion.
Salan runs for his life.

Salan has to think.
How can he kill the lion without
his sword or his sling?

He looks in his bag and sees his cloak.
Then he sees how he can kill the lion!

Salan climbs into a tree.
He drops his cloak on to the lion's head.

He jumps on to the lion's back.
He snaps the lion's neck with his hands.
Then he skins the lion and puts the
skin in his bag.

Salan has the lion's skin.
He will take it to the King.
Then soon, he will be free.

Quiz

Text comprehension

Literal comprehension
p3 What task does the King set Salan?
p11 How does Salan defeat the Lion of Jedda?

Inferential comprehension
p3 Why did the King set Salan this task?
p4 Do you think others had tried to kill the Lion of Jedda?
p6 Why do you think Salan cannot kill the lion with his sword or his sling?

Personal response
- Do you think Salan is brave or foolish?
- Do you think the King will grant Salan his freedom?

Word knowledge

p6 Find a word that means 'strikes'.
p8 Find a word made of two words.
p11 Which verb describes how Salan breaks the lion's neck?

Spelling challenge

Read these words:

take   with   she

Now try to spell them!

Ha! Ha! Ha!

Why do lions eat raw meat?

Because they don't know how to cook!

Find out about

- lions in Africa that kill and eat humans.

Tricky words

- humans
- man-eaters
- workers
- slept
- fences
- terrified
- waited
- closer

Read these words to the student. Help them with these words when they appear in the text.

Introduction

Lions that kill and eat humans are called man-eaters. In Africa in 1898, two man-eaters killed workers while they slept. In those days people used to shoot lions if they killed people, so a man called John Patterson went after the lions with his gun. The lions turned on him but he managed to shoot them just in time.

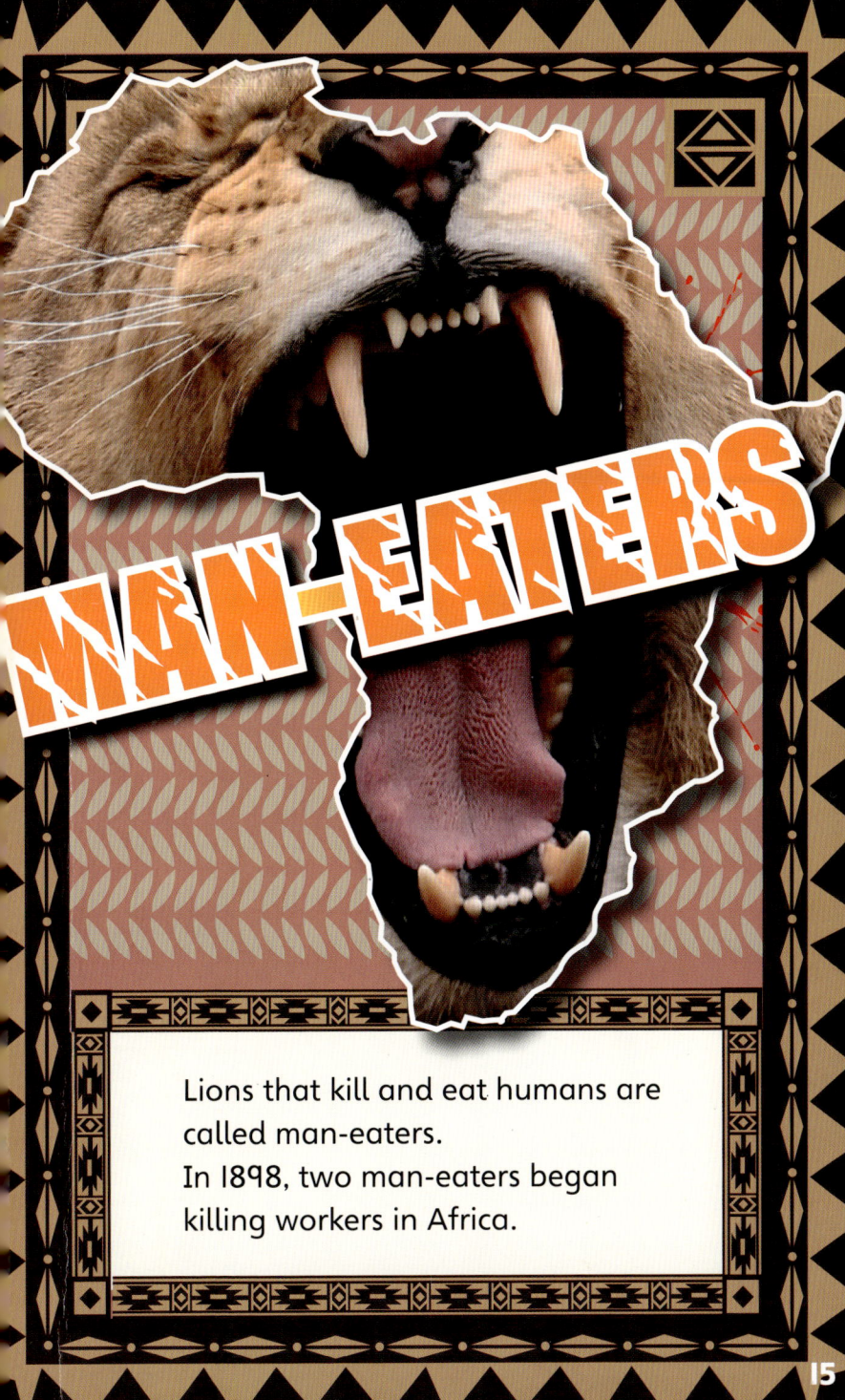

MAN-EATERS

Lions that kill and eat humans are called man-eaters.
In 1898, two man-eaters began killing workers in Africa.

The lions came into the workers'
camp at night.
They killed some workers as
they slept.

Night after night the lions came
back to the camp.
The workers made fires to keep
the lions away.
They made fences to keep the
lions away.

But it was no good.
The lions came back and the killing went on.
The terrified workers began to run away.

But a man called John Patterson
went after the lions.
Night after night he waited for
them with his gun.

Then at last he saw one of the lions.
But the lion saw John and came after **him**!
The lion came closer and closer.
John took aim and shot it dead.

John waited and waited to get
the other man-eater.
Then, at last, he saw it.
He took aim and shot at it.
But the lion did not stop.
It just came after him.
John was terrified.

John shot the lion in the chest.
But the lion did not stop.
It just came closer and closer.
John had time for one last shot.
He shot the lion in the head
and killed it.

The man-eaters were dead.
The workers came back to the camp.
John had saved them.

Quiz

Text comprehension

Literal comprehension
p15 What are man-eaters?
p17 What did the workers do to keep the
   lions away?

Inferential comprehension
p18 Why did it matter if the workers ran away?
p21 Why do you think John Patterson was terrified?
p23 Do you think the workers thought John Patterson
   was a hero? Do you?

Personal response
• Do you think it is right to shoot man-eaters?
• Why might some lions become man-eaters?

Word knowledge

p15 Why does the word 'Africa' have
   a capital letter?
p18 Find a word that means very scared.
p20 Why is the word 'him' in bold?

Spelling challenge

Read these words:

just   here   going

Now try to spell them!

Ha! Ha! Ha!

On which day do lions eat people?

Chewsday!